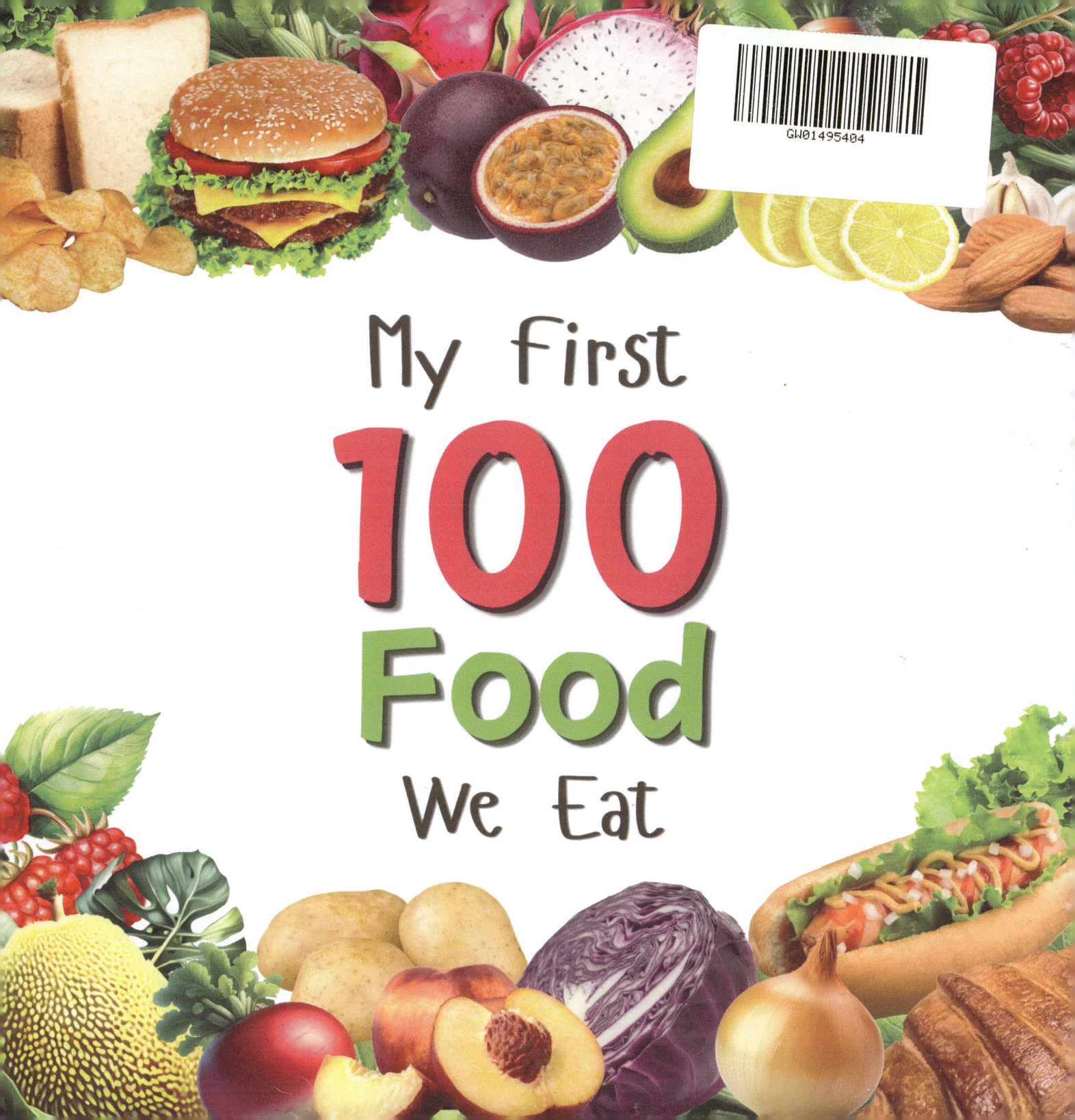

My First 100 Food We Eat

by Jam Nana

Lychee

Small Radish

Kiwi

Beet

Mango

Coconut

Pomegranate

Fig

Fried Chicked

Sandwich

Butter

Salmon

Mangosteen

Beef

Red Orange

Shrimp

Sweet Potato

Chocolate

Lollipop

Moon Cake

Red Grapes

Cranberry

Peach

Cornflakes

Pea

Eggplant

Purple Cabbage

Almond

 Churro	 Backberry
 Papaya	 Honey

Avocado

Popcorn

Cheese

Sliced Bread

 Olives	 Dragon Fruit
 Orange Juice	 Yogurt

Cupcake

Rice

Lettuce

Egg

Guava

Strawberry

Pancake

Roasted Chicken

Cherries

Berries

Green Apple

Burger

 Quince	 Broccoli
 Lemon	 Watermelon

Chocolate Cookies

Pasta

Potato

Spaghetti

Zucchini

Radish

Banana

Fusilli

Passion Fruit

French Fries

Raspberry

Pizza

 **Gac Fruit**	 **Macaroon**
 **Cookie**	 **Pineapple**

Pumpkin

Hot Dog

Bread

Dried Apricots

Nacho Chips

Bell Peppers

Red Apples

Chip

Rosella Fruit

Walnut

Grape

Vegetable Soup

Iceberg lettuce

Waffle

Spinach

Tomato

 Tamarind	 Salad
 Cucumber	 Salsa

Ice Cream

Nimki

Tea

Jackfruit

 Corn	 Onion
 Carrot	 Garlic

Thank You
for your order

by Jam Nana

Printed in Dunstable, United Kingdom